The Authoring Cycle:

A Viewing Guide

To literacy learning

The Authoring Cycle:

A Viewing Guide

edited by

JEROME C. HARSTE
KATHRYN MITCHELL PIERCE
TREVOR CAIRNEY

Heinemann Educational
Books
Portsmouth, N.H.

HEINEMANN EDUCATIONAL BOOKS INC.
70 Court Street, Portsmouth, New Hampshire 03801
London Edinburgh Melbourne Auckland
Hong Kong Singapore Kuala Lumpur
New Delhi Ibadan Nairobi Johannesburg
Kingston Port of Spain

© *Indiana University Foundation 1985*
First published 1985
ISBN 0-435-08222-1

Printed in the United States of America
Design by Wladislaw Finne

This viewing guide accompanies the videotape series:
THE AUTHORING CYCLE:
READ BETTER, WRITE BETTER, REASON BETTER

A Collaborative Project Between:

Language Education
Learning Resources
Radio & Television Services

Indiana University

Hosted & Developed by:

Jerome C. Harste
Language Education

Produced & Directed by:

Ed Jurewicz
Radio & Television Services

Distributed by:

Heinemann Educational Books

Contents

PREFACE vii

INTRODUCTION 3

VIEWING GUIDE 11
(*Overview, Key Points, Quotable Quote, Follow-Up Activities, Suggested Readings*)

Tape 1—A Natural Curriculum 11
Tape 2—The Authoring Curriculum 14
Tape 3—A Classroom for Authors 17
Tape 4—Taking Ownership 20
Tape 5—Authors' Circle 23
Tape 6—Editors' Table 26
Tape 7—Celebrating Authorship 29
Tape 8—Extending the Cycle 32

WORKSHOP STRATEGY LESSONS 39

Tape 1—Written Conversation 39
Tape 2—Sketch to Stretch 40
Tape 3—Say Something 42
Tape 4—Picture Setting 44
Tape 5—Authors' Circle for Teachers 47
Tape 6—Editors' Table for Teachers 49
Tape 7—Book Making 51
Tape 8—Cloning an Author 53

VIEWER SUPPORT MATERIALS 59

Series—The Authoring Cycle Song 59
Tape 3—Say Something Handout 60

Tape 5—Strategy Lesson Handout: Authors' Circle 62
Tape 5—Student Stories for Authors' Circle 65
Tape 6—Strategy Lesson Handout: Editors' Table 69
Tape 6—Student Stories for Editors' Table 75
Series—Biographical Sketches: Guest Experts 80

Preface

This Viewing Guide accompanies the videotape series, *The Authoring Cycle: Read Better, Write Better, Reason Better*. It has been divided into three sections and has been designed to support the viewer prior to, immediately after, and in the weeks following the viewing of each of the videotapes making up the series.

The first section contains a conceptual introduction to the series, an overview of each program including key points, a quotable quote (set in italic type between rules), follow-up activities, and suggested readings.

The Workshop Strategy Lesson section is included for the convenience of workshop leaders. This section contains a detailed lesson plan for one activity that viewers might engage in after viewing each videotape. These strategies are based upon, but extend, the strategies which viewers will have seen on the videotape. Workshop support materials are included in the Viewer Support Materials section of this Guide. If viewers have a personal copy of this Viewing Guide, no duplication of these or other materials is needed.

In the Viewer Support Materials section viewers will find a brief biographial sketch of the guest experts appearing in the series, the words to the Authoring Cycle Song, and student stories which they will need in conjunction with some of the suggested follow-up activities.

In addition the authors of this Viewing Guide are in the process of preparing an extensive teacher's handbook. This handbook will include a written description of how the authoring cycle works in classrooms, and lesson plans for each of the strategy lessons referred to in the series. Teachers will find this handbook a handy resource as they attempt to set up an authoring cycle in their classrooms.

In addition to these resources, viewers may wish to use a textbook in conjunction with this videotape series to build background information on language and language learning. For this purpose we suggest *Language Stories and Literacy Lessons* (Harste, Woodward, Burke, 1984). In this book the conceptual principles underlying the authoring cycle are established using protocol examples from child as informant research.

Introduction

The Authoring Cycle:
Read Better, Write Better, Reason Better

In the final analysis our interest in reading and writing is an interest in learning. In terms of what the mind does, researchers studying the process of reading and the process of writing have found that both processes have much in common. Even more importantly from an educational perspective, they have found that both reading and writing support the process of learning.

Figure 1 summarizes many recent insights into the reading and writing process by suggesting that:
1. Reading and writing are events which involve the making and shaping of ideas in time and space;
2. Cognitively, both reading and writing are driven by a search for a unified meaning, or "text;"
3. In this search for a unified meaning, readers and writers begin with what they know, but in this process learn, that is, go beyond what they know;
4. Readers and writers do this by constantly shifting perspectives from reader to writer, from speaker to listener, from participant to spectator, from monitor to critic, during the process of reading and writing;
5. There is in this sense no "pure" act of reading or writing—writers talk, read, write, listen, draw, gesture, all in the name of writing; readers discuss ideas they find problematic, listen, sketch, underline and do a number of other things, all in the name of reading;
6. The multimodal and social nature of reading and writing make these processes complex events, but the very com-

plexity of these events supports learning by allowing language users to shift perspective from reader to writer, speaker to listener, experiencer to spectator, spectator to critic;

7. In their specific detail, reading and writing vary by the circumstances of use. For example, there are differences in function and form between journals and letters, letters and stories, stories and poetry;

8. To be successful, readers and writers must orchestrate form and function to create a text which permits themselves and others to take the mental journey, or lived-through experience, our society defines as 'literacy' in a given context of written language in use.

The Authoring Cycle: Read Better, Write Better, Reason Better builds upon these insights but takes them one step further by addressing the issue of instruction. The question that this videotape series answers is one teachers ask, namely, "What are the instructional implications of what we recently have come to understand about the relationship among reading, writing, and reasoning?"

Figure 1: The Authoring Cycle

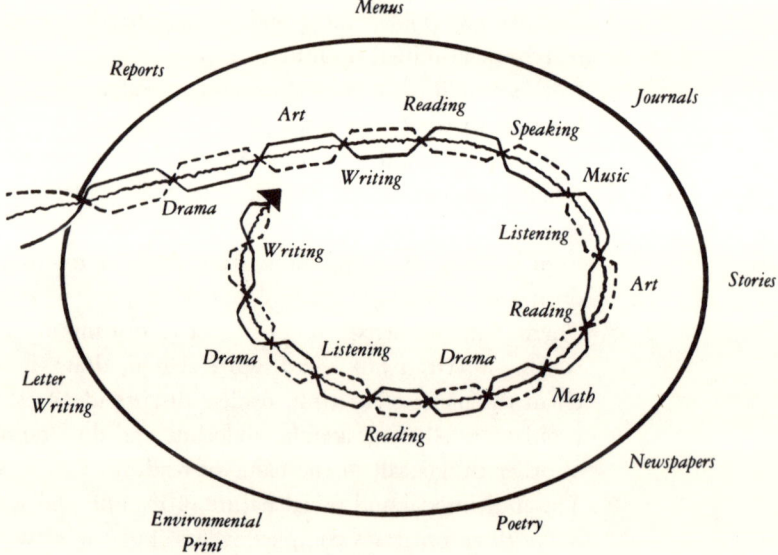

4   *The Authoring Cycle: Read Better, Write Better, Reason Better*

To answer that question the videotape series takes the model in Figure 1 and moves it to a curricular frame (Figure 2). The series poses curriculum as that place where theory and practice transact. Given what we currently know about literacy, literacy learning, and teaching, new theory—what Michael Herzfeld calls "practical theory"—evolves.

The contribution which this videotape series makes is that it gives teachers a curricular frame—an authoring cycle—around which they can plan curricular experiences and thus gain and give children a perspective on literacy not available before. This is a significant contribution, as curriculum is what falls through the cracks in all too many current approaches to reading and writing instruction. We are lesson plan oriented when instruction should be more broadly structured upon the learning process. Because this charge can be made of skill programs as well as of many whole language programs, teachers holding various theoretical perspectives can gain new perspectives on literacy and the teaching of literacy from viewing this series.

Figure 2: The Authoring Cycle as a Curricular Frame

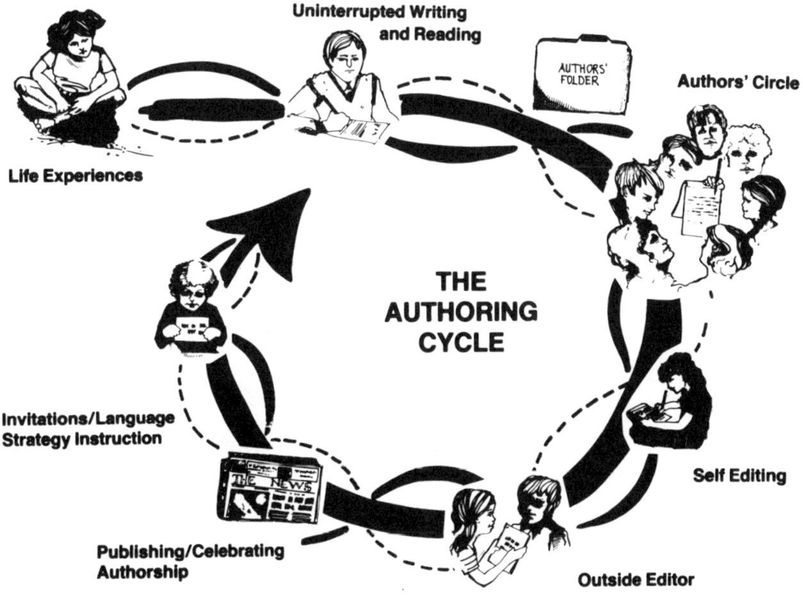

THE AUTHORING CYCLE

- Life Experiences
- Uninterrupted Writing and Reading
- Authors' Circle
- Self Editing
- Outside Editor
- Publishing/Celebrating Authorship
- Invitations/Language Strategy Instruction

Using the authoring cycle as an organizational device, individual videotapes in this series present a reading and writing curriculum developed by Carolyn Burke, Jerome C. Harste, and some teachers, as we worked collaboratively at setting up a comprehension-centered reading and writing program that would reflect what we currently know about literacy and literacy learning. You will meet Carolyn Burke and the teachers involved— Myriam Revel-Wood (4th grade, University Elementary School, Monroe County Community School Corporation), Mary Lynn Woods (W.R.I.T.E., a multi-aged summer reading and writing program, Eagle-Union Public Schools), and Sue Robinson (6th grade, School 39, Indianapolis Public Schools)—in the videotape and activities presented. However, we have borrowed freely from many other practicing teachers and researchers who have been attempting to do exactly what we did.

As a function of seeing these teachers in action in their classrooms viewers come to understand, at a practical level, how the supportive language arts teacher can create an environment in which language users can experience, see demonstrated, and come to value the strategies we associate with successful language use and learning. Viewers walk away not only with strategy lessons that they can implement on a Monday morning, but also with the knowledge of how to organize these instructional activities into a curriculum using the authoring cycle as their frame.

Tape 1—*A Natural Curriculum* introduces what we currently know about literacy and literacy learning in and out of school. Strategy lessons in this videotape show how teachers might build instruction naturally upon these experiences and this knowledge base.

Tape 2—*The Authoring Curriculum* introduces the notion of reading and writing as mental events which occur over time in a socially supportive environment. Strategy lessons in this videotape demonstrate how oral language, art and other communication systems can be used to support authoring in reading and writing.

Tape 3—*A Classroom for Authors* addresses specifically how teachers might go about more effectively organizing for instruction given our current knowledge base. Strategy lessons in this videotape are designed to help teachers create a classroom environment which is conducive to both authors and authorship.

Tape 4—*Taking Ownership* shows how teachers, building on the child's personal experience, can get the authoring process started in both reading and writing. Strategy lessons in this videotape demonstrate how teachers might use reading as an invitation to writing, and vice versa.

Tape 5—*Authors' Circle* demonstrates how authors support authors in the process of reading and writing. Strategy lessons in this videotape illustrate how teachers support language users by helping them shift perspectives from writer to reader, from author to audience.

Tape 6—*Editors' Table* gives teachers and children a more functional perspective on literacy. Strategy lessons in this videotape address the issue of convention and demonstrate how teachers, children, and curriculum might more effectively approach convention by placing it in the perspective of an authoring cycle.

Tape 7—*Celebrating Authorship* illustrates how publishing and publication are not the end of the authoring cycle but opportunities to start the cycle anew. Strategy lessons in this videotape show a variety of practical devices for celebrating authors and authorship which teachers and children can explore and use in their classrooms.

Tape 8—*Extending the Cycle* shows how the authoring cycle as a curricular frame can be extended for use in content areas like social studies and science. Strategy lessons in this videotape walk teachers through a unit of study demonstrating how the cycle works and how strategy lessons might be combined to form curriculum. Teachers and children are helped to see reading and writing not as ends in themselves, but as vehicles for learning.

Viewing Guide

1
A Natural Curriculum

OVERVIEW

Everyone seems interested these days in how to improve the teaching of reading and writing. In this program theoretical alternatives are presented. The implications of child language research for curriculum are discussed and demonstrated. Building on what is currently known about reading, writing, and learning, a more functional curricular base is proposed. (30 min.)

Guest Experts: Martha King, Carolyn Burke, Donald Graves, Diane DeFord, Kittye Copeland, Robert J. Tierney, Mary Lynn Woods, Dorothy Watson, Kenneth Goodman (see Biographical Sketches: Guest Experts in Viewer Support Materials section).

Field Footage: Strategy Lessons—*Peanut Butter Fudge, Written Conversation.*

KEY POINTS

- For children and adults alike, language is a functional tool. The impulse to reach out, to communicate with others, to use language to explore and expand our world is part of the human condition.
- Children are capable and willing language learners.
- What a teacher believes about language and language learning is important.
- Teaching and learning are not one and the same; all that a child knows has not been taught; what is taught may not be what is learned.

- There is nothing more basic in language than meaning.
- The natural curriculum encourages exploration of language through language.
- Learning language, both in school and out of school, requires a language rich environment.
- The natural curriculum preserves the wholeness and meaningfulness of language.
- In their specific detail reading and writing vary by the circumstances of use.
- Reading and writing are complex social events which involve multiple systems of communication in addition to language.

"Children seek to communicate, to reach out through language to further explore and expand their world."

—M.A.K. Halliday

FOLLOW-UP ACTIVITIES
- See *Written Conversation* and *Cloning an Author* in Workshop Strategy Lessons section.
- Collect some of the environmental print your students encounter frequently. Brainstorm with a partner some ways of incorporating in your curriculum the out-of-school experiences your children have with language.
- List all of the things that you would do if you only had more time. Weigh this against what you are doing with the time you have. Discuss ways in which you can reorganize your classroom to avoid a "stop-and-go" curriculum.
- Ask your students to keep a learning log at the end of each day. After one week, examine which learning experiences seem most salient to them.
- Become a kid watcher. Observe children at play in a home situation. Record some of what they are learning.

SUGGESTED READINGS
Bussis, A. M. (December, 1982). " 'Burn it at the cas-

ket' Research, reading instruction, and children's learning of the first R." *Phi Delta Kappan*, 60:1, 237–241.

DeFord, D. E. (September, 1981). "Literacy: Reading, writing and other essentials." *Language Arts*, 58:6, 652–658.

Goodman, K. S. (September, 1983). "The solution is the risk: A response to 'A Nation at Risk.' " *SLATE Newsletter*. Urbana, IL: National Council of Teachers of English. (Reprinted in *Education Digest*, January, 1984).

Goodman, K. S. (1984). "Unity in reading." In A. C. Purves & O. Niles (Eds.), Becoming readers in a complex society: 83rd yearbook of the National Society for the Study of Education (Part I). Chicago, IL: University of Chicago Press.

Goodman, Y., & Burke, C. (1980). "A reading curriculum: Focus on comprehension." Reading strategies: Focus on comprehension. New York, NY: Holt, Rinehart & Winston.

Harste, J. C., & Burke, C. A. (1979). "Understanding the hypothesis, It's the teacher that makes a difference." Reading horizons: Selected readings. Kalamazoo, MI: Western Michigan University.

Harste, J. C., & Burke, C. A. (1980). "Toward a sociopsycholinguistic model of reading comprehension." In B. Farr & D. Strickler (Eds.), Reading comprehension: Handbook to accompany reading comprehension videotape series. Bloomington, IN: 211 Education Building, Indiana University.

Harste, J. C., Siegel, M., & Stephens, D. (1985). "Toward a practical theory of literacy and learning." In A. Petrosky (Ed.), Reading and writing: Research and theory. Norwood, NJ: Ablex.

Holdaway, D. (1979). The foundations of literacy. Portsmouth, NH: Heinemann Educational Books. (Also available from Ashton Scholastic.)

Watson, D. J. (1982). "What is a whole-language reading program?" *The Missouri Reader*, 7:1, 8–10.

Sherman, B. W. (November, 1979). "Reading for meaning." *Learning*, 60:1, 41–44.

2
The Authoring Curriculum

OVERVIEW

From a process perspective reading and writing involve composing. As readers and writers search for a successful text given a particular context, they speak, read, write, listen, take notes, sketch, and in general take natural advantage of literacy as an event in time. Understanding this "authoring cycle" provides teachers with a much-needed conceptual frame whereby they can organize and plan more viable curricular experiences for children. (30 min.)

Guest Experts: Yetta Goodman, Carolyn Burke, Glenda Bissex, Nancy Shanklin, Robert J. Tierney, P. David Pearson, Donald Graves, Myriam Revel-Wood, Sue Robinson, Dorothy Watson, Olga Scibior (see Biographical Sketches: Guest Experts in Viewer Support Materials section).

Field Footage: Strategy Lessons—*Say Something, Sketch to Stretch, Choose Your Own Adventure.*

KEY POINTS

- The process curriculum returns the students to the center of the curriculum.
- The process curriculum enables us to view learning as an event and a matter of growth over time.
- The process curriculum must be something that our students experience and not something that we administer.
- The process curriculum must support the child in experiencing, valuing, and expanding the very process by which we mean.

- The "real" curriculum is what goes on in the mind of the student.
- The teacher's role is best seen as one of support of—not intervention in—the process.
- The authoring cycle provides a vehicle for structuring the classroom environment so that children are continually engaged in the kinds of mental activities which we associate with successful written language learning and use.
- The authoring cycle places curriculum development in the hands of the teacher, where it has always belonged; it places curriculum in the head of the child, where it has always been.
- Language literacy involves the ability to successfully use language as a vehicle for exploring and expanding your world.
- The very complexity of language supports successful language use and learning.

"I don't like using the notion of a reading and writing curriculum because to me, really, reading and writing are tools . . . they're tools to learning, and that's why I think we have to focus on the total experience in the school."

—Yetta Goodman

FOLLOW-UP ACTIVITIES

- See *Sketch to Stretch* in Workshop Strategy Lessons section.
- Immediately after viewing this videotape take 5 minutes to "free write." Put down your thoughts about what was presented. Write continuously, do not stop to worry about spelling, punctuation, or which words to use. Let your thoughts flow freely. Exchange your free write with a friend, being mindful that it is much easier to intimidate a language user than it is to support one. Discuss how you felt sharing your first draft efforts with one another. Discuss the implications of your experience for teaching.
- Create a 3 column observation form by labeling the respective columns "Experiencing," "Coming to Value"

and "See Demonstrated." Observe a classroom language arts lesson. From the perspective of the learners involved, record what they learned about language relative to each of these categories. Share your observations with other workshop participants.
- What do we stand to gain or lose by shifting our stance from using materials and tests as our curricular informants to using children as our curricular informants? What changes up and down the curriculum would such a shift in perspective entail?
- Record your time schedule each day for a week. Write down the time at which each new activity begins and ends, and the nature of that activity. During the second week, record the same information for one child, noting the child's activities and the times when these activities change. Compare the class time schedule with an individual child's schedule. How does the overall time schedule cover up the individual experiences of each child? What insights into our curriculum are to be gained by considering the activities of one child?

SUGGESTED READING

Baghban, M. (1984). Our daughter learns to read and write: A case study from birth to three. Newark, DE: International Reading Association.

Bissex, G. L. (1980). GNYS AT WRK: A child learns to write and read. Cambridge, MA: Harvard University Press.

Cohn, M. (May, 1981). "Observations of learning to read and write naturally." *Language Arts*, 58:5, 549–555.

Ferreiro, E., & Teberosky, A. (1982). Literacy before schooling. Portsmouth, NH: Heinemann Educational Books.

Goodman, Y. (1978). "Kid watching: An alternative to testing." *Journal of National Elementary School Principals*, 57:4, 22–27.

Harste, J. C., Woodward, V. A., & Burke, C. A. (1984). "Examining instructional assumptions." Language stories

& literacy lessons. Portsmouth, NH: Heinemann Educational Books.

Heath, S. B. (1983). *Ways with words.* Cambridge, England: Cambridge University Press.

King. M., & Rental, V. (1979). "Toward a theory of early writing development." *Research in the Teaching of English,* 13:1, 243–253.

Scibior, O. (Fall 1984). "Transactional processes in literacy learning: Toward a reconsideration of the concept 'strategy;' " *Forum in Reading and Language Education,* 1:1, 3–26. (Order from 211 Education Building, Indiana University, Bloomington, IN 47405.)

3
A Classroom for Authors

OVERVIEW

In the final analysis our interest in reading and writing is an interest in learning. Reading and writing are dynamic processes which involve the maintenance, generation, and exploration of learning both in ourselves and with others. Classroom conditions which mitigate against children experiencing what real literacy is all about are identified. By providing children with choice, by creating a low-risk environment, and by organizing classrooms around the various contexts of literacy, we can do much to make classrooms more natural language learning environments. (30 min.)

Guest Experts: Glenda Bissex, Vera Milz, Nancy Shanklin, Martha King, Carolyn Burke, Donald Graves, Myriam Revel-Wood, Sue Robinson, Dorothy Watson, Orin

Cochran (see Biographical Sketches: Guest Experts in Viewer Support Materials section).

Field Footage: Strategy Lessons—*Message Board, Journals, Pen Pals, Uninterrupted Reading and Writing.*

KEY POINTS
- Text is more than the physical phenomenon of ink on paper.
- Both the reader and the writer are involved in the creation of meaning.
- Both the reader and the writer approach new encounters with language based on past encounters with language.
- The classroom must provide functional opportunities for children to explore reading and writing.
- Children need to come to understand that function and form in language vary by circumstances of use.
- Authority must give way to authorship in language instruction.
- When children read and write daily, they begin reading like a writer and begin writing before they are writing.
- Choice is an integral part of the learning process.
- Children can only learn a process through involvement in that process.
- Risk taking is central to language use and learning.

"Parents have always helped children to learn to use language by paying attention to what the child is talking about. This suggests, then, in classrooms that we stand back from the language and we pay more attention to the learning environment."

—Martha King

FOLLOW-UP ACTIVITIES
- See *Say Something* Strategy in Workshop Strategy Lessons section.

- Reading and writing function as tools in teaching and learning. How might your daily timetable be altered to allow uninterrupted time to use reading and writing in the subject areas you teach?
- Reading and writing must have a purpose. Examine the daily operation of your classroom looking for ways that functional reading and writing might play a role.
- One way that we demonstrate our values is by reading and writing ourselves, in front of our students. What opportunities do you provide for students to see you reading and writing? What additional opportunities exist that you might take advantage of?
- Reading and writing play an important role in our lives. Help your students to develop interviews with adults in the school and the community to identify the ways in which reading and writing are used.

SUGGESTED READINGS

Buchanan, E. (Ed.). (1980). For the love of reading. Winnipeg, Manitoba: The C.E.L. Group. (Order from Orin Cochran, 14 Regula Place, Winnipeg, Manitoba R2W 2P9.)

Harste, J. C., & Carey, R. F. (1984). "Classrooms, constraints, and the language process." In J. Flood (Ed.), Promoting reading comprehension. Newark, DE: International Reading Association.

Milz, V. (1980). "The comprehension-centered classroom: Setting it up and making it work" (Videotape). In D. J. Strickler (Producer & Director), Reading comprehension: An instructional videotape series. Bloomington, IN: 211 Education Building, Indiana University.

Rhodes, L. K. (1983). "Organizing the elementary classroom for effective language learning." In U. H. Hardt (Ed.), Teaching reading with the other language arts. Newark, DE: International Reading Association.

Shanklin, N. K. L. (1981). Related reading and writing: Developing a transactional theory of the writing process (Monograph in Language and Reading Studies).

Bloomington, IN: School of Education Publications Office, Indiana University.

Smith, F. (1981). "Demonstrations, engagement and sensitivity: A revised approach to language learning." *Essays into literacy.* Portsmouth, NH: Heinemann Educational Books.

Tierney, R. J., & Pearson, P. D. (May, 1983). "Toward a composing model of reading." *Language Arts,* 60:5, 568–579.

4
Taking Ownership

OVERVIEW

We make children tenants, not owners, of text. We have to help children take charge of the process. We do this by providing time, building from personal experience, encouraging variability, and receiving and respecting first draft efforts. Rather than reducing literacy to a set of rules for spelling and grammar, we should help children, through their involvement with authors and in the authoring process, to develop a more functional view of literacy. As a result of lived-through curricular experiences, children come to re-value the processes of reading and writing—or literacy more generally—as involving the manipulating and shaping of ideas in time and space. (30 min.)

Guest Experts: Donald Graves, Martha King, P. David Pearson, Vera Milz, Nancy Shanklin, Kittye Copeland, Carolyn Burke, Myriam Revel-Wood, Sue Robinson, Dorothy Watson, Rudine Sims (see Biographical Sketches: Guest Experts in Viewer Support Materials section).

Field Footage: Strategy Lessons—*Getting to Know You, Picture Setting, Extended Literature Activities.*

KEY POINTS
- Practicing writers write with meaning and purpose; practicing readers read with meaning and purpose.
- Children have to see clear relationships between the reading and writing they do in school and reading and writing as it occurs in the outside world.
- Children will develop a sense of ownership if what they read and write evolves out of their own interests and world knowledge.
- Meaning in reading and writing begins with personal experience. There is no other place from which sense-making can begin for language users.
- Curriculum builds from and extends the natural strategies of language learning that children bring with them to school.
- In both reading and writing, the first draft efforts of children and adults often bear more in common than is generally assumed.
- Teachers encourage ownership by setting up a supportive environment which allows children to get in touch with, and come to value, their own personal feelings and worlds.
- Reading and writing in good classrooms occurs with purpose and direction. Purpose and direction come not from the dictates of the teacher, but from involvement in the authoring cycle as we theoretically know it and instructionally support it.
- Children need to experience and come to value reading and writing as vehicles for shaping ideas in time and space.

"It has to be a classroom in which children matter . . . and that means that we are willing to begin where the children are, regardless of what 'curriculum' might be out there."

—Nancy Shanklin

FOLLOW-UP ACTIVITIES

- See *Picture Setting* in Workshop Strategy Lessons section.
- Children's literature plays a central role in a comprehension-centered reading and writing program. Begin to develop your own list of favorite books. Discuss possible ways to extend each book. What invitations would you make?
- Start an Author's Club. To begin select a favorite author and identify all of his or her works. Have each person in the club select one of the author's books to read. Meet to discuss and share the books you have read. Identify what you see as the primary traits of this author and his or her writing style. Select another author and keep the club going.
- Brainstorm with a small group all the uses to which reading and writing are put in your everyday lives. Select two or three of these uses and work together to create a classroom situation where reading and writing can serve similar functions.
- Many commercially published language arts programs include units on letter writing. Look at the events planned for your classroom to see where letter writing might serve a functional purpose.

SUGGESTED READINGS

Pearson, P. D., & Tierney, R. J. (1984). "On becoming a thoughtful reader: Reading like a writer." In A. C. Purves & O. Niles (Eds.), Becoming readers in a complex society: 83rd yearbook of the National Society for the Study of Education (Part I). Chicago, IL: University of Chicago Press.

Langer, J. A., & Smith-Burke, M. T. (Eds.). (1982). Reader meets author/bridging the gap. Newark: DE: International Reading Association.

Newman, J. M. (October, 1983). "On becoming a writer: Child and teacher." *Language Arts*, 60:7, 860–870.

Rhodes, L. K. (February, 1981). "I can read! Predictable books as resources for reading and writing instruction." *Reading Teacher*, 34:6, 511–518.

Sims, R. (1980). Children's literature in a comprehension-centered reading program (Videotape). In D. J. Strickler (Director & Producer), Reading comprehension: An instructional videotape series. Bloomington, IN: 211 Education Building, Indiana University.

Smith, F. (1983). "Reading like a writer." *Language Arts,* 60:1, 558−567.

Tompkins, J. P. (1980). "An introduction to reader-response criticism." In J. P. Tompkins (Ed.), Reader-response criticism. Baltimore, MD: Johns Hopkins University Press.

Turbill, J. (Ed.). (1982). No better way to teaching writing! Rozelle, N.S.W.: Primary English Teaching Association. (Distributed by Heinemann Educational Books, Portsmouth, NH.)

5
Authors' Circle

OVERVIEW

Every encounter with language affords language users the opportunity to learn language, learn about language, and learn through language. The very first reader that a writer encounters is him or herself. Authors' Circle socially supports the process by providing composers with a critical, but supportive, second audience. Through the process of sharing, children are given the opportunity to shift perspectives and to take a new look at their composition. Understanding the process real readers and writers follow allows children to see and experience revision for what it really is, namely, semantic editing or "re-vision." (30 min.)

23 *Viewing Guide*

Guest Experts: Nancy Shanklin, Carlolyn Burke, Glenda Bissex, Donald Graves, Kittye Copeland, Mary Lynn Woods, Myriam Revel-Wood, Dorothy Watson, Paul Crowley (see Biographical Sketches: Guest Experts in Viewer Support Materials section).

Field Footage: Strategy Lessons—*Authors' Circle, Conferencing.*

KEY POINTS
- Reading and writing are the vehicles through which we document our thoughts in the present and preserve them for the future.
- As writers, we also function as readers—the first reader any writer will encounter is herself/himself.
- Because reading and writing are events that evolve over time, the experiences of reading and writing themselves have an impact on what we learn.
- What we read or write can have as much influence in reformulating our thoughts and emotions as our thoughts and emotions have on what we read or write.
- Semantic revision—the refinement of ideas in time and space—is at the heart of both the authoring and learning processes.
- Anyone can intimidate language learners; few truly know how to support them.
- As readers and writers we use those about us to support us in the process.
- The authoring circle functions as a community of readers and writers working jointly to support each other.
- The structure of the authoring cycle is simple and predictable—the direction that the discussion will take is not, though ownership must never be an issue.
- In seeing their text through the eyes of an audience readers and writers confirm strategies that are successful while being made aware of those that are not.

"It's that shift in perspective in writing, approaching what I've just written, or am in the process of writing, as a reader, that gives me strategies that are available from the reading process that are not immediately available from the writing process."

—Carolyn L. Burke

FOLLOW-UP ACTIVITIES
- See *Authors' Circle for Teachers* in Workshop Strategy Lessons section.
- Explore reading in the writing process by trying "blind writing." Insert a piece of carbon paper between two blank sheets and staple all three together. Using a pen which no longer writes, a sharpened dowel or stick, or a typewriter without a ribbon, try writing when you are unable to see what you have produced, i.e., when reading has been removed from the writing process. (It's not fair to squint at the impressions your writing instrument has left behind!) Now read what you have written by examining the carbon after you have finished. Take 5 minutes and free write on this experience.
- After you have viewed this videotape take out a sheet of paper and write a retelling which includes some of your reactions to the piece. Put your written retelling away. Within the next couple of days write a new retelling without consulting your original. Compare your second version to the original. If time permits view the videotape again.
- A "language story" is something real that happens in the life of a language user in which an important principle of language or language learning is highlighted. Start a collection of language stories or vignettes. Encourage a colleague to support you in your writing by forming an Authors' Circle.
- Select a first-draft piece of writing to read (one of the Student Stories for Authors' Circle, see Viewer Support Materials section, may be used if no other first-draft piece of writing is immediately available). Think of 10 positive and supportive things to say about it.

SUGGESTED READINGS

Bingham, A. (1982). "Using writing folders to document student progress." In T. Newkirk & N. Atwell (Eds.), Understanding writing. Chelmsford, MA: Northeast Regional Exchange.

Calkins, L. M. (December, 1980). "The craft of writing." *Teacher*, 60:1, 41–44.

Calkins, L. M. (1983). Lessons from a child. Portsmouth, NH: Heinemann Educational Books.

Graves, D. H. (1982). Writing: Teachers and children at work. Portsmouth, NH: Heinemann Educational Books.

Harste, J. C. (September, 1981). "Holy squirrel." In J. Harste & L. Rhodes (Series Eds.), Making Connections through language stories column, *Language Arts*, 58:1, 627–630.

Sowers, S. (1982). "Reflect, expand, select: Three responses in the writing conference." In T. Newkirk & N. Atwell (Eds.), Understanding writing. Chelmsford, MA: Northeast Regional Exchange, pp. 76–90.

6
Editors' Table

OVERVIEW

When an author decides to take a manuscript to publication, it is edited for convention in order to show the author's regard for readers. Being an editor is different from being a writer. The editing process consists of a semantic editing followed by an editing for convention. Semantic editing by outside readers focuses only on identification of portions of text which seem unclear or confusing. Editing for convention highlights the notion that control of conventions is not a prerequisite to production of meaningful messages, but a final stage for manuscripts that the author chooses to make public. Serving as editors of one another's texts helps children develop an appreciation of audience and the communicative commitment they make to their readers. (30 min.)

Guest Experts: P. David Pearson, Carolyn Burke, Kittye Copeland, Vera Milz, Mary Lynn Woods, Myriam Revel-Wood, Dorothy Watson, Carole Edelsky (see Biographical Sketches: Guest Experts in Viewer Support Materials section).

Field Footage: Strategy Lesson—*Editors' Table*.

KEY POINTS

- In a very real sense we are never finished with our writing because we are never finished thinking.
- Undue emphasis on the mechanics of language too early in the process can stop a child's writing before it ever gets a chance to get started.
- Editors support writers by helping them say what it was they meant to say in the first place.
- All writers need editors. Good readers often socially edit their understanding of text by saying something about their understanding to other readers.
- Meaning, not convention, is the place where readers and writers meet in text.
- Getting the meaning straight is what drives the editing process.
- Being an editor does not give one the right to assume ownership of the piece being edited.
- The process of editing in both reading and writing has been occurring long before editing is highlighted in the authoring cycle.
- A good language arts curriculum ought to provide opportunities for language users to change perspectives in the authoring cycle, from reader to writer, from participant to critic, from critic to monitor.
- Readers actively edit and self-edit as they reread past texts in light of the current text that they are reading.

"I think one of the problems in a lot of schools is that we give students the notion that when texts are finished they ought to be letter perfect and kids don't realize that texts are never finished—at some point you just stop writing."

—P. David Pearson

FOLLOW-UP ACTIVITIES
- See *Editors' Table for Teachers* in Workshop Strategy Lessons section.
- Observe a teacher go over a piece of writing with a student, or "edit" the meaning of a story through class discussion with a group of learners. On one side of your observation form list what the teacher taught. On the other side of your observation form list what it was that you think the child learned.
- Return to the free write you did in the early days of the workshop. Reread what you have written. Write a revision based on your deeper understanding of the topic. Share your revision with a partner, asking for their reactions and questions. Revise again for clarity. Ask someone to edit the piece for you.
- Language permits us to reflect upon our thoughts as well as upon language as a system unto itself. As you watch children edit other children's work, begin to make notes in a journal of the instances in which these students comment upon language itself. Discuss with a partner the curricular implications of what you have learned.
- Growth in language use occurs slowly, over time, and is evidenced in small steps. Reconsider your present evaluation system and look for ways in which it could be expanded to include evaluations over time. What new record keeping procedures would such a move entail?

SUGGESTED READINGS
Beers, C. S., & Beers, J. W. (May, 1981). "Three assumptions about learning to spell." *Language Arts*, 58:5, 573–580.

Black, J. (September, 1981). "Those 'mistakes' tell us a lot." *Language Arts*, 57:5, 508−513.

Daigon, A. (December, 1982). "Toward righting writing." *Phi Delta Kappan*, 60:1, 242−246.

Edelsky, C., & Smith, K. (January, 1984). "Is that writing—or are those marks just a figment of your curriculum?" *Language Arts*, 61:1, 24−32.

Gannon, P. (1982). "Responding to children's writing." In R. Carter (Ed.), Linguistics and the teacher. London: Routledge & Kegan Paul.

Graves, D. H., & Giacobbe, M. E. (May, 1982). "Questions for teachers who wonder if their writers change," *Language Arts*, 59:5, 495−503.

Perl, S. (1979). "The composing process of unskilled college writers." *Research in the Teaching of English*, 13:2, 363−369.

Zutell, J. (February, 1979). "Spelling strategies of primary school children and their relationship to the Piagetian concept of decentration." *Research in the Teaching of English*, 13:1, 69−80.

7
Celebrating Authorship

OVERVIEW

Sequels and second editions of books testify to the fact that publishing is often not the end, but rather the start of the authoring cycle. Books and children go together. Children need opportunities to meet a variety of fiction and non-fiction authors, see their classmates as authors, and come to see themselves as authors. Children who write read differently. Good writers live off, but celebrate in, the

29 *Viewing Guide*

interpretation and reinterpretation of their literary heritage. Good readers read texts in the light of past texts. Celebrating authors and authorship is not enrichment but an integral component of the curricular cycle. (30 min.)

Guest Experts: Donald Graves, Mary Lynn Woods, Myriam Revel-Wood, Yetta Goodman, Carolyn Burke, Vera Milz, Susan Robinson, P. David Pearson, Robert Tierney, Dorothy Watson, Patricia Jenkins (see Biographical Sketches: Guest Experts in Viewer Support Materials section).

Field Footage: Strategy Lessons—*Young Authors' Conference, Author's Chair, Readers' Theater.*

KEY POINTS
- All children need to experience the joys of publication and authorship.
- A primary motivation for writing is to reach out and communicate to others.
- Not everything written should be published; some pieces ought to be abandoned; others have served their purpose in helping us think through an issue at the point of first draft.
- The purpose of publication is to celebrate authorship not artifacts; to celebrate authorship is to celebrate the future; to celebrate artifacts, the past.
- Publishing helps bridge the gap between what we do and what others do in the name of literacy; it, in this sense, helps children assume membership in "the club."
- Children need to explore a variety of publishing outlets in the classroom.
- Publication documents our growth as writers as it testifies to our having achieved ownership of the writing process.
- Student publications are as much real literature as are professionally published trade books and must be treated as such in the classroom.
- Children's literature plays a key role in developing a comprehension-centered reading and writing program.
- Because reading supports the writing process from

invention through publication it is, in its own right, an important form of celebrating authors and authorship.

"It's actually 'Young Author's Conferencing'; the publishing is really a very minor part . . . It honors the child that is enjoying writing and bringing it to a published form."
—Vera Milz

FOLLOW-UP ACTIVITIES
- See *Book Making* in Workshop Strategy Lessons section.
- Select a children's author or illustrator you particularly enjoy. Develop a unit through which you share this author or illustrator with your class, involving them in a variety of ways with the artist's work. Encourage your students to develop a similar unit for a favorite author or illustrator to share with their classmates.
- Consider the ways in which various types of children's writing might be shared. Brainstorm within a small group alternative modes of presentation that might be appropriate for different audiences.
- Nancy Shanklin talks of moving to alternate forms of communication—art, movement, drama, music. Select a favorite theme or topic and explore the alternate forms you might use in presenting aspects of this topic. How might you encourage your students to make use of alternate forms in presenting their understanding of the topic?
- One way that teachers can support one another is by creating a sharing library. Place photocopies of articles which have been particularly useful to you in a file folder with a check-out card. Invite other teachers to check out articles from your collection and to contribute articles which they have found particularly useful.

SUGGESTED READINGS
Rhodes, L. K., & Hill, M. W. (1983). "Home-school cooperation in integrated language arts." In B. A.

Busching & J. I. Schwartz (Eds.), Integrating the language arts in the elementary school. Urbana, IL: National Council of Teachers of English.

Black, A., & Comber, B. (1983). " 'I can rit.' Knowing where children are in their writing development." In J. Anderson & K. Lovett (Eds.), Teaching reading and writing to every child. Rozelle, N.S.W.: Australian Reading Association. (Order from P.O. Box 187, Rozelle, New South Wales, Australia, 2039.)

Graves, D. H., & Hansen, J. (February, 1983). "The author's chair." *Language Arts*, 60:2, 583–592.

Rosenblatt, L. (1982). The reader, the text, the poem. Carbondale, IL: Southern University Press. (Also available from the National Council of Teachers of English, 1111 Kenyon Road, Urbana, IL 61802.)

Scales, P. (1982). Dial-an-author: How to develop a successful reader-writer interview program. New York, NY: Bantam Books. (Order brochure from School & College Department, 666 Fifth Avenue, New York, NY 10103.)

Trelease, J. (1982). The read-aloud handbook. New York, NY: Penguin Books.

8
Extending the Cycle

OVERVIEW

Reading and writing are vehicles by which we explore and expand our world. The authoring cycle, rather than being a reading and writing curriculum *per se*, gives teachers a curricular frame around which they can plan content area experiences. In a real sense reading and writing are the core of any curricular area of study. In this sequence, the authoring cycle is used to demonstrate reading and writing across the curriculum. In so doing, new curricular invitations are made as we come full circle. (30 min.)

Guest Experts: Carolyn Burke, Donald Graves, Susan Robinson, Myriam Revel-Wood, Kittye Copeland, Yetta Goodman, Nancy Shanklin, Martha King, Dorothy Watson (see Biographical Sketches: Guest Experts in Viewer Support Materials section).

Field Footage: Strategy Lesson—*Reading and Writing Across the Curriculum.*

KEY POINTS

- A process curriculum is an instructional framework **grounded in** our current understanding of the learning process.
- A comprehension-centered reading and writing program highlights new insights and sets new goals for the language arts as it accents reading, writing, reasoning relationships.
- A process approach to curriculum accents the language process and its relationship to the learning process.
- Effective authors select strategies as a function of whom they are attempting to communicate with, how they are attempting to communicate and what they are attempting to communicate.
- Language learning is a function of the quality of, not the quantity of, language encounters.
- All learning involves doing; that means we learn about by learning through, and that teachers have to value the learner as being active, responsible, and having a significant contribution to make.
- Teachers and children must view reading and writing not as subjects, but as vehicles for discovery; the tools of learning.
- Reading and writing are tools for learning. In this sense there ought not to be a "reading and writing curriculum" *per se.*

- The authoring cycle provides a framework for organizing classrooms so that children are engaged in learning language through learning through language.

"A lot of people assume that . . . if kids do a lot of reading, it'll feed into their writing and if they do a lot of writing it'll feed into their reading . . . What I think is more interesting is to adopt a perspective that reading and writing are both composing."

—Robert J. Tierney

FOLLOW-UP ACTIVITIES
- See *Cloning an Author* in Workshop Strategy Lessons section.
- We "offer a language curriculum" all the time, whether we plan for it or not. What are some aspects of language that we are teaching by the way we choose to teach mathematics and science?
- Plan an integrated unit with a small group. Select a first-hand experience that can be shared (e.g., raising chickens, planning a pet show) and brainstorm ways to explore and learn from this experience. List language invitations which will allow children to think about and reflect upon this experience.
- Teachers do not work in isolation. Teacher support groups are forming across the nation as teachers work to make changes in their classrooms. Work with a small group to generate a list of the ways that a support group might be useful to you as you contemplate "extending" your own learning.
- Brainstorm ways in which you might involve parents more effectively in your classrooms. Discuss in what ways parent involvement extends the authoring cycle.
- Write a letter to the President of your local council of the International Reading Association. Suggest that they host a Young Authors' Conference in your community. Include a

rationale in which you explain how such programs extend the school curriculum and are in the self-interests of professionals in reading and language education.

SUGGESTED READINGS

Atwell, M., Block, J., & Modesatt, M. (1983). Learning in college: Integrating information. Dubuque, IA: Kendall Hunt.

Barnes, D. (1975). From communication to curriculum. New York: NY: Penguin Books.

Bransford, J. D., & Stein, B. S. (1984). The ideal problem solver. New York, W. H. Freeman.

Cleland, C. J. (March, 1981). "Highlighting issues in children's literature through semantic webbing." *Reading Teacher*, 60:1, 642–646.

Copeland, K. (1982). "Content areas/language arts: Should they be separated?" *The Missouri Reader*, 7:2, 11–12.

Crafton, L. K., Hill, M. W., House, A. L., & Kucer, S. B. (1980). "Language instruction: From theoretical abstraction to classroom applications." Occasional Papers in Language and Reading. Bloomington, IN: 211 Education Building, Indiana University.

Newman, J. M. (February, 1984). Language learning and computers. *Language Arts*, 61:5, 494–497.

Norton, D. E. (November/December, 1977). "A web of interest." *Language Arts*, 54:8, 928–932.

Revel-Wood, M. (September, 1981). Science clubs. *Science and Children*, 60:1, 21–23.

Shuh, J. H. (Spring, 1979). "Writing our own story." *Journal of Education*, 60:1, 1–10.

Workshop
Strategy Lessons

1

Written Conversation

Developed By: Carolyn Burke

Written By: Jerome C. Harste, Kathryn Mitchell Pierce

INTRODUCTION

This activity is designed to make workshop participants aware of the close relationship between writing and reading. *Written Conversation* provides an informal atmosphere in which workshop participants are encouraged to explore meaning with each other. While attention to conventions arises from a need to make one's meaning clear, the informal atmosphere in which the writing is taking place gives priority to the meaning of the exchange.

MATERIALS/PROCEDURES

- Overhead projector, markers, blank acetates
- Paper and pencils

Using the overhead projector, the workshop leader begins a public written conversation with a workshop participant over the content of the videotape. After a few exchanges, workshop participants are asked to pair up and engage in a similar "conversation."

Note Each exchange ends in the asking of a question.

WORKSHOP LEADER'S ROLE

Given the nature of this workshop, after introducing the activity, workshop leaders should continue to engage in written conversations with one or two of the workshop participants, depending on how the pairing of workshop participants works out. To conclude this activity leaders should pull the group together for purposes of sharing the various topics the pairs discussed and the conclusions that they reached. These points can be put on an overhead.

FOLLOW-UP

Written conversation can be combined with most other activities as a vehicle for workshop participants to discuss either plans for carrying out some activity or what they've understood from some reading or writing experience.

Participants should be encouraged to try this activity with their own students in their own classroom.

2
Sketch to Stretch

Developed By: Jerome C. Harste, Marjorie Siegel, Karen Feathers

Written by: Jerome C. Harste

INTRODUCTION

Sketch to Stretch helps language users realize that there are many communication systems by which we create meaning. The activity develops insight into language as a communication system by helping workshop participants see that explaining what they know is easier when they can use more than one method of communicating. It makes clear that interpretation is open and subjective, based on prior knowledge and experience.

Sketch to Stretch encourages workshop participants to go beyond a literal understanding of what they have experienced. Workshop participants who are reluctant to take risks or who have dysfunctional notions of language see that not everyone has the same response to a selection. When they are given the opportunity to explain what they have drawn, meaning (whether or not it is the other workshop participant's meaning or not) is rendered understandable. Participants are pushed to explore aspects of meaning they may have captured in art that they were not cognizant of having understood verbally.

MATERIALS/PROCEDURES

- Pencil, paper, colored magic markers

After viewing the videotape, workshop participants are asked to think about what was said and then draw a sketch of what the experience meant to them. They are told there are many ways of representing the meaning of an experience and they are free to experiment with their interpretation. When the sketches are done, each person in the group shows his/her sketch to the others. Participants in the group are asked to study the sketch and say what it is they think the artist is attempting to say. The artist, of course, gets the last word. Sharing proceeds in this fashion.

WORKSHOP LEADER'S ROLE

The leader's role in this strategy is to help the students focus on interpretation rather than on their artistic talents. Leaders should do their own *Sketch to Stretch* and share it in a group just like the rest of the workshop participants. To conclude this activity acetate sheets may be distributed and one sketch from each group may be shared with the entire workshop membership. At some point a discussion should highlight how different background experiences lead to different interpretations of text.

FOLLOW-UP

Sketches can be compiled and later put into a Class Composed Book (See *Book Making* Strategy.)

Participants can be encouraged to include sketches along with their written work, particularly projects, in order to expand on the interpretation being presented.

This strategy can also be used in writing. After a first draft (or when writer's block is experienced) workshop participants can be asked to shift to another communication mode. No priority should be given to moves to art. Participants can be asked how else they might represent their meaning, and their choice of pantomime, drama, math, music, can be honored. Participants should return to writing once they have expressed their meaning in an alternate mode.

Participants should be encouraged to use this strategy with their own students as an alternative to traditional reading comprehension activities or when students in their class seem to be experiencing writer's block.

3
Say Something

Developed By: Jerome C. Harste, Carolyn Burke, Dorothy Watson

Written By: Jerome C. Harste

INTRODUCTION

Language did not develop because of the presence of one language user but because of the presence of two, who wished to communicate. Language and language learning are inherently social events. *Say Something* highlights the social nature of language and demonstrates that understanding develops and evolves from our interactions with others. Participants are able to see that "partnership" enhances meaning, and that as constraints normally operating in reading are altered so are involvement and the kind of thinking that becomes possible.

Workshop participants are encouraged to explore interpretation and the relationship between what they have learned in the past and what is offered in the present reading selection. As a function of their involvement in this process participants will develop new insight into the reading process and why it is that the only place that any language user can begin to make sense of a reading experience is in terms of his or her own background of experience.

MATERIALS/PROCEDURES

- *Say Something* Handout (see Viewer Support Materials section)
- Overhead projector, clear acetate, overhead pens

Viewers are asked to choose a partner and locate the *Say Something* Handout in their Viewing Guide. Before reading, each pair of participants decide how they will read (orally or silently). Participants are told to read a paragraph and then stop to "say something" to their partner about what they have read. After one partner has said something, it is the second person's turn to "say something" about what they have read. After this exchange the partners read the second paragraph and then "say something" to each other before going to the third paragraph and so on through the text.

WORKSHOP LEADER'S ROLE

Leaders should identify a partner and participate in *Say Something* along with the group. Once the majority of participants have finished reading the selection, the leader should organize a group discussion by writing "Constraints that operate in classroom setting" in the middle of an overhead, circling it twice, and then ask participants to talk about what constraints the author talked about in this article. As constraints are mentioned, examples of what they mean should be solicited as the leader webs the various constraints participants talk about on the overhead.

After a group discussion centering on the content of the article, the leader should engage participants in a discussion of: (1) how *Say Something* facilitated reading comprehension (what processes were used and how these helped), and (2) how *Say Something* as an activity differs in terms of constraints from, say, the typical kind of teacher questioning that occurs in classrooms after reading instruction. Answers to each of these questions can be recorded on an overhead for purposes of focusing the discussion.

FOLLOW-UP

Written Conversation may be combined with *Say Something* by having participants conduct written conversations with other partners about their reading and reactions.

Participants should be encouraged to use *Say Something* with the students in their classroom or whenever it is that they encounter something particularly difficult to understand in their reading.

4
Picture Setting

Developed By: Stephen Kucer, Carolyn Burke

Written By: Jerome C. Harste

INTRODUCTION

Picture Setting provides a starting point for workshop participants to identify a topic of personal interest that they might write about and thus create their own text. Events such as flying a kite on a windy day, a Sunday drive with the family, or roller skating around the neighborhood (as opposed to *"The* Trip to California") may acquire new potentials and significance for authors. Asking participants to go home and invest some time in looking through magazines for a picture setting they might use permits them to experience and be actively involved in authoring; that is, "writing" before they actually start writing. By beginning in an alternate communication system, participants get in touch with their feelings and what this experience meant to them. The time spent choosing the setting, drawing the characters, and sharing what they are thinking about, gives participants an opportunity to think through their story, plan, and find the activities themselves supportive of the authoring process.

MATERIALS/PROCEDURES

- A wide choice of pictures for settings (pictures without people or animals)
- Various 8½" × 11" pieces of construction paper
- Stapler
- 3" × 3" pieces of construction paper, scissors, tape, crayons
- Paper and pencils

Workshop participants are asked to go home and look through magazines to identify a picture of a setting that reminds them of an *important* moment in their lives, disregarding whether they believe others would see it as significant or not. If participants forget to bring in their picture, they may look through and select a picture from the pile you have provided. This picture becomes the setting for their story.

Using the 3" × 3" pieces of construction paper, participants are asked to draw and color the characters involved in this experience. Thinking about the color of the clothes that various persons were wearing is an important part of the experience in that it often helps put writers in touch with their feelings and emotions. Characters are colored, cut out, and moved around on the picture as the students orally share what they were thinking about writing with a fellow workshop participant. After this experience participants should be given uninterrupted time for writing.

WORKSHOP LEADER'S ROLE

Workshop leaders should identify 2 or 3 pictures of settings that remind them of moments that hold personal importance yet to others might seem rather insignificant. Participants should be asked to select pictures that are background settings only, devoid of characters. Only experiences which can be publicly shared should be identified.

As participants bring in their picture settings, these should be trimmed and mounted using a stapler on pieces of 8 ½" × 11" construction paper. To get the project underway, leaders should invite selected participants to hold up their picture and share what it was they were thinking about writing. Leaders should then invite participants to draw a picture of the characters involved in their story, discussing with them the importance of color and its relationship to meaning and human significance. Once participants have their setting and characters another sharing time can occur. Participants then should be invited to write and be given plenty of time to do so. The leader should at this time also write and as the writing progresses casually talk with students as they work, encouraging them to discuss their setting, the characters, and their stories up until this point. Leaders should receive these pieces and keep all discussions open-ended by asking participants where they see their piece going from this point. To conclude the activity leaders may ask a group of 2 or 3 participants to share their pictures, characters, and rough drafts with the group.

FOLLOW-UP

Participants can be asked to find pictures of people or objects that remind them of particular experiences.

Participants would then draw the setting before writing their stories.

Rather than identifying settings that remind them of a personal experience, participants can be asked to find settings that they think would make a good backdrop for a fictional story. Leaders might suggest this option to any participants who seem to have difficulty identifying a personal experience which they might share.

The rough draft that participants create will be brought to *Authors' Circle* and used as an initial piece to walk participants through The Authoring Cycle. Participants can be asked to create "An Author's Folder" using a manilla file folder in which to keep their rough draft work.

5
Authors' Circle for Teachers

Developed by: Carolyn Burke

Written by: Jerome C. Harste, Kathryn Mitchell Pierce

INTRODUCTION

Anyone can intimidate a fellow language user; what is needed are opportunities for learning how we can support fellow readers and writers. In this activity workshop participants walk through *Authors' Circle* learning how they might receive student writing and identifying what responses are and are not so helpful.

MATERIALS/PROCEDURES

- Participants bring to *Authors' Circle* the rough draft copies of the texts they created in *Picture Setting*

- Pencils (to take notes on suggestions offered by fellow participants in *Authors' Circle*)
- If participants do not have their own rough drafts, copies of Student Stories for *Authors' Circle* (see Viewer Support Materials section) may be used for purposes of simulating this experience.

After viewing the videotape, participants should be invited to form groups of 3 or 4 and walk their way through *Authors' Circle* based on their current level of understanding. Participants should be reminded that their role is to support their fellow language users and that ownership of the piece must remain in the author's hands at all times.

Once one of the participants in each group has experienced *Authors' Circle*, a sharing time should follow in which problems and statements that were and were not helpful might be discussed. After this discussion, participants should be asked to locate the Strategy Lesson Handout: *Authors' Circle* (see Viewer Support Materials section). Participants should be asked to peruse this document, identify both the most and least successful parts in their experience of conducting *Authors' Circle*, and then proceed to walk their way through *Authors' Circle* in their groups.

WORKSHOP LEADER'S ROLE

Workshop leaders should participate in an *Authors' Circle* of their choice.

If participants do not have their own rough draft texts to take to *Authors' Circle* viewers will need to locate the Student Stories for *Authors' Circle* in their Viewing Guide. Participants should be asked to get into groups of 4 for purposes of simulating *Authors' Circle*. One of the 4 stories should be assigned to each participant. Participants should be asked to assume that this is their own story for the purposes of the simulation. As a culminating experience, participants may be called together and asked to generate a set of guidelines or principles that they might follow in conducting *Authors' Circle*.

FOLLOW-UP

Using the Student Stories for *Authors' Circle*, participants can be asked to say 10 good things about each piece of writing prior to giving one suggestion for how the piece might be improved.

Viewers should be encouraged to set up the authoring cycle in their classrooms.

6

Editors' Table for Teachers

Developed by: Carolyn Burke

Written by: Jerome C. Harste

INTRODUCTION

Teachers need to understand the supportive role that editors play in the writing process. This activity allows teachers to experience firsthand the process of editing and learn how they can support students in the writing process by setting up an *Editors' Table* in their classroom.

MATERIALS/PROCEDURES

- Revised copies of *Picture Setting* Stories
- If participants do not have their own rough drafts of texts to send to *Editors' Table*, Student Stories for *Editors' Table* (see Viewer Support Materials section) may be used for purposes of simulating this experience

- An *Editors' Table* area should be designated and set up in the workshop area (see Strategy Lesson Handout: *Editors' Table* in Viewer Support Materials section for a list of materials)

After viewing the videotape, selected participants should be asked to play the role of class editors and walk their way through the editing process as they currently understand it.

Once one story has been edited, a sharing time should follow in which problems are discussed. After this discussion, participants should be asked to locate the Strategy Lesson Handout: *Editors' Table* in the Viewer Support Materials section. Participants should be asked to read this document, identify what they need to do differently, and then proceed to handle a second piece at *Editors' Table*.

WORKSHOP LEADER'S ROLE

Workshop leaders should organize participants in groups of 4. If participants do not have their own revised rough drafts to send to *Editors' Table*, workshop leaders should help participants locate Student Stories for *Editors' Table* in their Viewing Guide.

As a culminating experience participants should be called together and asked to generate a set of guidelines to follow in conducting *Editors' Table* in their respective classrooms.

FOLLOW-UP

Participants can be asked to design their own *Editors' Table* for their classroom addressing specifically what items they would have available and where in the classroom it would be located. Plans should be shared and discussed.

Teachers should be encouraged to set up an *Editors' Table* in their own classrooms.

7
Book Making

Developed by: Vera Milz
Written by: Jerome C. Harste

INTRODUCTION

Celebrating authorship is an important component of the authoring cycle. To make the authoring cycle work in the classroom a publication program is needed. Having a ready supply of blank books for student use encourages authorship and makes involvement in the authoring cycle a functional activity. This activity introduces teachers to an easy procedure for making durable and attractive blank books for use in their classrooms.

MATERIALS/PROCEDURES
- Rolls of contact paper (18 books per roll)
- Regular sized typing paper
- Sewing machine
- Rubber cement
- Scissors
- Cardboard (1 empty cereal box per book)

1. Stack and fold in half 6 pieces of typing paper. Stitch down the middle using a sewing machine set on the widest stitch possible.
2. Cut two pieces of cardboard measuring 6 × 9 inches from front and back of cereal box.
3. Cut a piece of contact paper 11 × 15 inches.

4. Center the two cardboard pieces on the sticky side of the contact paper, leaving ¼ inch between the two pieces so the book will close (see illustration). Fold in the 4 corners of the contact paper, sticking them to the exposed cardboard pieces. A dot drawn in the middle of each corner will serve as a guide in folding. (The outside corners of the contact paper should be aligned with the dots.) Fold all remaining contact paper over the edges of the cardboard to complete the book cover.
5. Place the stitched pages so that the stitching runs between the two cardboard pieces. To ensure a permanent bond, apply rubber cement to the entire surface of the book cover. While this is drying, apply cement to the outside of the front cover of the book. Allow both to dry completely. Then carefully place the cement coated book page onto the front cover. Repeat process to adhere the back page to the back cover.

WORKSHOP LEADER'S ROLE

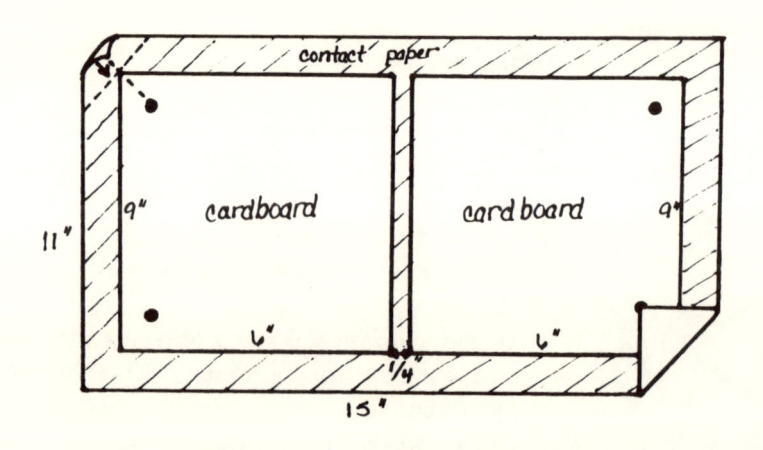

Leaders should make a book before the workshop begins. Participants should be given the materials and directions and told to make a book. Do not try to anticipate their problems, as any difficulties can be discussed as they occur.

FOLLOW-UP

Have participants type a final copy of their *Picture Setting* stories and rubber cement these pages into the book. Illustrate with drawings or photos to finish.

8
Cloning an Author

Developed By: Jerome C. Harste

Written By: Jerome C. Harste

INTRODUCTION

Successful reading and writing involve the creation of a text world where meaning is organized and unified. While each language user must take ownership of this process, teachers can support them in the process.

This activity focuses on creating a unified meaning, not necessarily the author's unified meaning. Participants "clone" the activities of an author, not the author herself or himself; hence the title of the activity is 'Cloning an Author' not 'Cloning the Author.'

MATERIALS/PROCEDURES

- Stack of ten 3" × 5" cards for each student
- Different colored cards, magic markers or highlighter pens can be bought and used by participants to identify sets of cards from different videotapes.

53 *Workshop Strategy Lessons*

Either during or after viewing each videotape, viewers are instructed to write what they see as the key concepts on 3"× 5" cards (words, phrases, sentences), putting one concept per card.

Participants are asked to look through their stack of cards and select what they see as the 7 major concepts they have recorded. (If you ask participants to throw 3 cards away they become actively involved in decision-making and in prioritizing key concepts.) Occasionally a participant may discover that a new card must be generated which more clearly captures the central theme.

Next, participants are asked to look through the 7 cards they have selected and pick out the one that most accurately summarizes the central theme of the videotape. This card they physically place in the center of a circle they imagine to exist on their desk or table top.

Once this card has been selected and placed, participants are asked to place the remaining cards around this card, such that their placement reflects how the participant saw these concepts interrelated and tied to this central concept and to each other in the selection they have read.

Working in pairs, participants take turns explaining to their partners why they selected the cards they did, and why they placed them as they did on their desks.

WORKSHOP LEADER'S ROLE

Workshop leaders should participate in this activity by identifying what they see as key concepts, laying out their cards, and sharing their cards with a partner.

FOLLOW-UP

Participants can pass their 7 card sets to new pairs of viewers. Once these participants have laid out the cards the' way they think makes the most sense, authors can share their organizational preferences. Authors may not insist that theirs is the correct organization, but rather should be encouraged to explore other organizational possibilities in their cards as demonstrated by the new pair's decisions.

Once two videotapes have been viewed, participants can be asked to take their 7 cards from Tape 1 and their 7 cards from Tape 2, shuffle them, and select 7 new cards from which to create a unified text which they can be asked to share with fellow participants. Using colored cards allows participants to get back to their original sets once they have engaged in this exercise.

Leaders are encouraged to engage participants in *Cloning an Author* after each videotape in the series. After Tape 8 is viewed all cards can be shuffled and participants asked to select the key 7 concepts for the whole series as a culminating activity. Results can either be shared orally or written in an uninterrupted writing session.

Viewers should be encouraged to use a similar card procedure with their students when they write reports. If they take 3" × 5" cards and record ideas from books they gather during library research, they can manually group the idea cards to facilitate writing organization.

In workshops where viewers have read a series of books or articles on a related topic, a similar procedure can be followed to encourage the creating of a unified meaning across selections. As a final experience in the workshop, viewers can be asked to identify one key card per videotape and write a summary of the workshop.

With kindergarten and early elementary aged children, students can be encouraged to write down or draw pictures of those things they want to remember as they read the story. Once they have done this they can put their cards in the order they wish and use them in retelling the story they read to their classmates. When we have used this activity with children, we have found retellings are not only much longer, but qualitatively much improved.

Viewer
Support Materials

The Authoring Cycle

Song

Words by: Jerome C. Harste

Music by: Randy Beard

It's mine, it's yours,
With you I'd like to share it,
'Cause as I share it with you,
You'll become an author too.

It's ours, help us celebrate,
We invite you now to share it,
'Cause if I share it with you,
I'll own it with you.

It's yours, but I can read it,
With you I'd like to share it,
'Cause if you share it with me,
I'll become an author too.

And if you have a draft to read,
If I have advice you need,
If you come to me and ask,
I'll edit with you.

It's ours, help us celebrate,
We invite you now to share it,
'Cause as we share it with you,
You'll become an author too.

3
Say Something Handout

Reference: Lee, D. M., & Rubin, J. B. (1979). "Language development." Children and language. Belmont, CA: Wadsworth, pp. 71-72. (Reprinted with permission from authors.)

Constraints School is an environment that influences all communication that takes place within it. Many teachers see their role as one that restrains their natural feelings and impulses. When they feel they must play a role not entirely natural to them, they are vulnerable to reactions of peers as well as those of the children. Children anticipate or "read" expectations of teachers that put severe constraints on their communication, limiting and modifying it. Children respond with an eye to the reactions of their peers also and often are caught in a dilemma between the two. How each child responds depends on his or her self-concept, the relationships already established with teacher, peers, and people in general, previous experiences in any similar situation, conception of what school is, and cultural and family background.

   Children often adopt resisting behaviors that are puzzling and disturbing to teachers. One boy read mechanically in a monotone because he felt reading with expression was "sissy.' Another group adopted two strategies: Either keep your mouth shut in class, or if you give the right answer, counteract the "fink effect" by sprinkling your response with stigmatized language.

   Teachers need to be aware of cultural differences and their

effect on children's reactions to the school situation. For instance, many cultures have an oral tradition in which reading and writing have little part. When children sense a lack of understanding or respect for their culture, they may feel that the dominant society is imposing its own culture through the requirements of the school. Thus, mutual distrust may build so that learning is minimized. It is important, therefore, that teachers try to avoid actions, words, and nonverbal signals that children may interpret negatively. Also, the way a school program is planned and carried out can help children to see school as an important and enjoyable experience.

The topic discussed and the function of that discussion also put restraints on a person's response. We are all aware that there are some subjects we discuss only with family and close friends, and some we discuss only with one friend. Some feel more constraints than others, but probably few ever feel completely free of any restraint past early childhood.

The way we express ourselves may be as restricted as the topic. Most of us have command of several language levels, including what has been called the "homey" or informal, "company" language, and perhaps formal speech for those who speak to groups in either prepared or spontaneous situations. Children quickly learn the difference between playground talk and classroom talk, between talking with peers and talking to the teacher. Whether these differences should exist and to what degree is a question deserving serious consideration and requiring an in-depth look at how the school creates this environment.

How what one says is received by others depends on many factors: the connotative as well as the denotative meaning of the words (do the words have special meanings to people because of past incidents?); the intonation, emphasis, and timing; other nonverbal aspects such as facial expression and body position and action; and the relationship already established between individuals involved.

5
Authors' Circle

Developed by: Carolyn Burke

Written by: Kathryn Mitchell Pierce, Jerome C. Harste

INTRODUCTION

Because every child's writing progresses at a different rate, not all children will be ready to attend an *Authors' Circle* at the same time. The *Authors' Circle* is made up of 3 to 4 children who have a piece they would like to share. This means that the piece has been edited by the author and deemed worthy, in his or her eyes, of moving to publication in some form. Each participant in the *Authors' Circle* must bring a piece to share—including the teacher. While the teacher doesn't need to participate in every *Authors' Circle*, he or she is encouraged to walk students through the process the first time they attend an *Authors' Circle*.

MATERIALS/PROCEDURES
- Pencil
- Rough draft copy of story
- Small round table or desks formed into circle

The first author reads his or her piece out loud to the authors attending *Authors' Circle*. Following this reading, each listener in the group "receives" the piece by explaining what he or she liked best about the piece. The discussion then returns to the author, who is asked, "What did you like the best about your piece?" "What parts have given you trouble in this piece?"

After the author responds to these questions—setting the topics for the discussion to follow—each listener has an opportunity to make suggestions to the author on the topics raised by the author. During this period the author makes notes on the recommendations but does not comment or defend his or her position.

The next author then reads his or her piece, continuing the process until each author has been heard, and has had an opportunity to respond to each piece brought to the group.

The authors then leave to consider, in private, the recommendations made and to arrive at their own decisions about changes. In order for students to maintain ownership of their own pieces, it is essential that this decision-making remain the responsibility of the author.

TEACHER'S ROLE

The teacher is free to make suggestions like other participants at *Authors' Circle,* but his or her recommendations must bear no more weight than any others. The teacher must develop a relationship with the students that allows them to feel free to reject a recommendation from the teacher.

Through participation in the first round of *Authors' Circle,* the teacher helps to set the tone for the exchanges. The goal is to create a supportive environment for authors. Comments which are unsupportive or which deal with aspects other than meaning should not be allowed. Similarly, comments which deal with portions of the story which the author himself or herself did not identify as problematic should be discouraged. Students should be reminded that it is easy to overwhelm an author with ideas. What we aim to do is give the author ideas, but permit the author to take the lead, and limit suggestions to only those things the author wishes to address.

FOLLOW-UP

Once the Authors' Circle pattern has been established, students may be encouraged to gather informally a few classmates to listen and respond to a piece. Even one or two listeners may be sufficient to suit an author's needs. In many instances, the authors will select students whose opinions they value.

As authors' pieces become lengthier, it may be necessary to provide copies of the drafts for each listener. This should only be considered after a tone has been set which focuses on content and not on convention.

5
Student Stories for Authors' Circle

OSIRIS by Alison

    Osiris was one of the most complex gods of acient Egypt. Osiris was believed to be the god of the underworld. His sister and wife Isis was the goddess of wheat and barly. His brother, Seth, was the demon of death. Osiris and Isis later had a son called Horus.
    Osiris was usually represented as a tightly wraped mummy with the hands comming out of the wrappings and holding the symbols of power, (the serpant and the eagle or hawk).
    Osiris was believed to have been a divine king who died by a trick played on him by his jelous brother Seth. It was believed that Seth had a beautiful coffon. He told the people that the person who fit in it would recieve it. Osiris jumped at the chance. Just as Osiris laid down Seth slammed on the cover and threw it into the Nile River. It was

that Osiris emerged from the waters to give the world life-giving plants Osiris was believed to have been taken apart and his parts scattered.

Osiris was worshiped in many places, but mainly in Abydos in Upper Egypt which was beleived to be the resting place of the head. It was believed that when a person died Anubis whould come and wheigh the heart against truth and justice. If it was lighter, the soul would become a star, if it was heavier, the sould would be left to torment in Osiris's chambers.

There was a play called "Mysteries of Osiris" which shows all of the struggles of Osiris.

All of the tales are so outlandish they are hard to believe. Even so, the Egyptions worshiped Osiris more than any other god. What do you think?

MY LIFE by Angel

I used to beat My head on the floor they thot my Mom beat me. When i became two i used to play in my cake. When i was three i used to pull hair. When i was for i was potty traned. I learn how to ride a bike. I used to fight when i was ten. I used

66 *Student Stories for Authors' Circle*

to be 11 and i used bad language and i used to get my mouth smaked from my mother. Now i 12, i still use bad language.

THE END of my life Angel

THE LONELY LEAF by Mudhi

The Lonely Leaf Mudhi

Once upon a time there was a Redbut tree it was the only tree in a little garden Then one day a big storm blew off all the leaves eccept one leaf and that leaf had Parents and feelings and the leaf was sad. It also was lonely. Then one day he heard on the radio that there was going to be a big, big storm and the leaf was so happy because he knew that he was going to fall off with his parents, But then he heard the radio say that there WASN'T going to be a storm after all. Now everybody was happy eccept that leaf. So he stayed all winter in that RedBud tree. But it was awfully cold and the leaf was so sad that he started to cry till winter was over then it became Spring and the leaves grew back on and that leaf was old and died.
The End

67 *Viewer Support Materials*

SAMMY THE SQUIRREL AND THE FOX by Dwayne

Sammy the squirrel, and the Fox   Dwayne

Once there was a squirrel named Sammy. He lived in a small oak tree in a very big forest in Indiana. A very mean and sly fox lived very near. The fox wanted revenge with Sammy because Sammy always escaped when the fox tried to catch Sammy. One time the fox was chasing Sammy Sammy looked ahead and saw a hole in the ground a few feet away. Sammy ran as fast as he could and went plunging in to the hole and fox ran smackin to a thorn bush OW cried the fox that was one time sammy had a good laugh. That day a Komodo Dragon escaped from the zoo! The Dragon walked by The fox. The fox said "hello". "What do you want" said the Dragon. "Well I have an extra room you could sleep in for the night," suggested the fox "and we could catch a squirrel for supper." "OK" said the Dragon. So the went out to catch Sammy. Sammy went down to the pond to get some seeds when the fox saw Sammy he ran as fast as he could.

The fox knew Sammy didn't like water so he would be traped. When they reached the pond Sammy jumped to the side and the fox went spashing in the pond. "I'll get you for this" yelled the fox as sammy ran up a tree. Sammy lived a very long life.

6
Editors' Table

Developed By: Carolyn Burke

Written by: Kathy Short, Jean Anne Clyde, Deborah Rowe

INTRODUCTION
Since the function of written language is to communicate a message, writers should focus on "getting their meaning down" during early stages of the writing process. However, when an author decides to take his or her manuscript to publication, it is edited for convention in order to show the author's regard for readers.

The editing process consists of both semantic editing and editing for convention. Semantic editing by outside readers focuses on the identification of those portions of the text which seem unclear or confusing. It extends the focus on meaning by encouraging authors to take another perspective on their writing. Editing for convention occurs after semantic editing to highlight the notion that control of conventions is not a prerequisite to production of meaningful messages. Instead it is a final concern for manuscripts that the author chooses to make public. After editing, the text goes to the typist who serves as a final check on conventions. The typist serves the same function that a secretary would for an employer.

The editing process provides a demonstration of an effective strategy used by published authors for dealing with aspects of convention. Serving as editors of one another's texts helps children develop an appreciation of audience and the communicative commitment they make to their readers.

This strategy is helpful for any writers who are taking their pieces to publication. It allows them to attend to meaning rather than be too concerned with conventions early in the process. It also helps them develop a personal strategy for self-editing and editing of others' texts.

MATERIALS/PROCEDURES
- Editors' table
- Editors' box for writers' drafts
- Blackboard or paper to write editing rules on
- Visors, armbands, buttons, etc., to identify editors
- Variety of regular and colored pencils or highlighter pens
- Scrap paper
- Dictionary, Spelling Dictionary, Thesaurus, English Style Book, and other reference materials as deemed useful
- Typewriter
- Overhead Projector
- Folders/ boxes for texts in process of being edited or typed
- Tape, scissors, rubber cement, and blank paper for pasting up galleys
- Copies of publications similar to those being published

1. Prior to establishment of an editorial board, it is important to establish a need for publication in the authoring cycle. Writers must have drafts which they have shared in an authors' circle. It is likely that authors will choose only some of the pieces they have written to go through the publication process.
2. Establish an editors' box in the classroom where students can place drafts that they want to have published and that have already gone through an authors' circle.
3. Ask for volunteers to serve as editors for the first publication. Have them submit their names in a box or folder and then draw names from this to determine who will serve as the first editors. It is helpful to include children of different ages and ability levels on the editorial board. This process will be repeated for subsequent publications so others have an opportunity to serve as editors. Decisions regarding length of board membership should be based on frequency and type of publication.
4. Call an editorial board meeting. You may want to distribute badges, visors, armbands, etc., to identify students during their terms as editors.
5. Examine and discuss published documents similar to the ones that the class will publish (e.g., trade books, newspapers, etc.). Ask what an editor does. The list should reflect the dual responsibilities of editors: editing for meaning and convention. During semantic editing, editors focus on meaning and are concerned that the text makes sense and that the meaning is clear. When they edit for convention they are concerned with spelling, punctuation, and capitalization. Semantic editing should always precede editing for convention. This will require several readings of each manuscript. Discuss text ownership by asking each editor to take a draft from the editors' box. Then ask the question, "Whose paper is this?" Clearly establish the idea that this is the author's text and that no one except the author has the right to change the meaning or structure of the text.
6. The teacher may wish to prepare a student text in

advance for use on the overhead projector to assist students in generating and applying editorial rules. It may be helpful if the editors each have a copy of that student text. Have the editors establish enough rules and symbols to enable them to begin the editing process. It is quite likely that other rules will evolve as the need arises. The list is always to be considered as a set of working guidelines which are subject to change, with adequate justification, by any subsequent editorial board. One of the participants serves as scribe, recording the suggestions (preferably on a chalkboard to emphasize the tentative nature of the decisions). Markings should be easily identifiable, yet small, so the author's manuscript is annotated as little as possible. It is helpful to devise a system that will make clear both what phase of editing a document is in and who is responsible so that questions can be easily referred to the appropriate person.

7. Post these rules in the editors' corner and continue to add and change them when suggestions are made by the editorial board.

8. Editing may not be necessary for all pieces in a publication or for all types of informal publications. The teacher and/or editors may decide to exclude some pieces from the editing process and print them as submitted (e.g., letters to the editors, artwork, personal ads, and other pieces whose original form is an integral part of the message).

9. Once the editorial board has decided on the rules and symbols they can begin the editing process.

   A. Semantic Editing: The editors' primary focus is identifying and marking with the agreed-upon symbols any portions of a text which require additional information to be understood, seem confusing, or need clarification. Stress the cardinal rule: No one has the right to alter the structure or meaning of a text except the author.

   B. Semantic Meeting: If questions regarding meaning arise, the editor must have a conference with the author. The editor should find the author, and ask him/her questions based on the semantic editing. The author decides whether or not he/she wants to make any changes and, if so, makes them during the conference.

C. Editing for Convention: Once all questions regarding meaning have been resolved with the author, the editor rereads the rough draft to edit for conventions such as spelling, punctuation, and capitalization. Highlighter pens can be used to mark words that the editor feels are functionally spelled (i.e., the author's current "best guess" at the word), and then to write the conventional spelling over the top of the word in question if it was found to be misspelled. If the editor is not sure of the conventional spelling, she or he might write out alternatives on a piece of paper, look it up in the dictionary, or consult with other editors including the teacher. If the editor is still unsure of the spelling, the word can be left underlined for the managing editor or final typist to deal with.

D. Typing of Manuscript: The manuscript is given to the typist, who may make final changes in spelling punctuation, or capitalization if nonconventional forms would embarrass either you, the child, or the school.

E. Editors' Conference: At the end of the first editing session, it is important for editors to regroup and discuss problems and issues that have arisen. This is a good opportunity to revise and add to editorial rules and policies.

TEACHER'S ROLE

The teacher needs to walk students through *Editors' Table*, making sure they understand the limits of their roles and responsibilities.

Teachers may serve as a spelling resource during editing for conventions.

The teacher is Managing Editor and in this role makes final decisions as to whether or not something will or will not be released for publication.

To make sure that publishing does not become the only goal of your reading and writing program, it is necessary for the teacher to establish the rule that only a given number of materials drafted (we recommend a maximum of 2 items per student per month) be taken through the authoring cycle. If students wish to publish more than this, they may do so on their own time at home.

FOLLOW-UP

When a second editorial board is established, procedures 1-5 may be repeated during the initial meeting. Because there already exists a set of editorial rules, step 6 will involve the sharing of current working rules for the editing process, rather than the generation of a new list. Former editors may be enlisted to explain existing policies. There should continue to be an emphasis on the tentativeness of these guidelines so that editors will feel comfortable in suggesting changes and refining policies.

Editors may find readers' comments useful in shaping their next publications. Re-examining an assortment of published materials may provide editors with ideas for responding to a wide range of reader requests. For instance, newspaper editors may receive requests for new types of articles, or for the addition of illustrations and artwork to make the document more interesting and appealing to readers. If publishing books, editors may receive suggestions concerning such features as a dedication or a table of contents. As the editors decide how to respond to such suggestions, they may wish to make new staff positions available in response to these reader-identified problem areas (e.g., cartoonists, artists, etc.).

Editing texts for publication is only one responsibility of editors. They may also be involved in making decisions about layout, organization of a collection of pieces, assembly and distribution of the publication, and/or types of future publications. As editors take responsibility for the entire publication process, it may be necessary to create specialized editorial positions to deal with these aspects of publication.

As the authoring cycle continues to operate over time and with various kinds of publications, the role taken by editors will change. The *Editors' Table,* as initially implemented, serves as a demonstration of editing to students. As they become familiar with the editing process, students gradually begin to self-edit and to informally edit with other authors.

More informal variations of the editing strategy may be used with different kinds of publications. Even in first grade, however, it is a good idea to have an Editors' Table in place so that children may take from 1 to 2 items per month through the cycle.

6

Student Stories for Editors' Table

OSIRIS by Alison

Osiris was one of the most complex gods of ancient Egypt. He was believed to be the god of the underworld. His sister and wife, Isis, was the goddess of wheat and barley. His brother, Seth, was the demon of death. Osiris and Isis had two sons, Anubis and Horus.

Osiris was usually represented as a tightly wrapped mummy with the hands coming out of the wrappings and holding the symbols of power (the serpent, and the winged bird). He was usually painted on the walls of tombs. Osiris was believed to have been a divine king who died by a trick played on him by his jealous brother Seth. It was believed that Seth had a beautiful coffin. He told the people that whoever fit in it would recieve it. Osiris jumped at the chance. Just as Osiris laid down Seth slammed on the cover and threw it into the Nile River. It was said that Osiris emerged from the water to give the world life-giving plants. Osiris was believed to have been taken apart and his parts scattered.

Osiris was worshiped in many places, but mainly in Abydos in Upper Egypt which was believed to be the resting place of the head. It was believed that when a person died Anubis would come and weigh the heart against truth and justice. If it was lighter, the soul would become a star. If it was heavier, the soul would be left to torment in Osiris' chambers.

There was a play called "Mysteries of Osiris" which shows all the struggles of Osiris.

All of the tales are so outlandish they are hard to believe. Even so, the Egyptians worshiped Osiris more than any other god. What do you think?

MY LIFE by Angel

I used to beat my head on the floor they thot (though) my Mom beat me. When I became two i used to play in my cake. When i was three i used to pull hair. When i was four (for) i was potty trained. I learn how to ride a bike. I used to fight when i was ten. I used to be 11 and i used bad language, and i used to get my mouth smaked from my mother. Now i'm 12, i still use bad language.

THE END of My Life Angel

When I was six.

THE LONELY LEAF by Mudhi

Once upon a time there was a Redbud tree it was the only tree in a little garden. Then one day a big storm blew off all the leaves eccept one leaf and that leaf had Parents and fellings and the leaf was sad. It also was lonely. Then one day he heard on the radio that there was going to be a big, big storm and the leaf was so happy because he knew that he was going to fall off with his parents. But then he heard the radio say that there W A S N ' T going to be a storm after all. [Leave a bigger space] Now everybody was happy eccept that leaf. So he stayed all winter in that Redbud tree. But it was awfully cold and the leaf was so sad that he started to cry till winter was over then it became Spring and the leaves grew back on and that leaf was old and died. [add this ∨]

(That leaf didn't have the baddest life in the world or the best in the world).

The End.

Student Stories for Editors' Table

SAMMY THE SQUIRREL AND THE FOX by Dwayne

Once there was a squirrel named Sammy. He lived in a small oak tree in a very big forest in Indiana. A very mean and sly fox lived very near. The fox wanted revense with Sammy becaus Sammy always escaped when the fox tried to catch sammy. One time the fox was chasing sammy, sammy looked ahead and saw a hole in the ground a few feet away. Sammy ran as fast as he could and went plunging in to the hole ;and fox ran smack in to a thorn bush O W cried the fox that was one time Sammy had a good laugh. That day a Komodo Dragon escaped from the zoo! The Dragon walked by The fox. The fox said "hello". "What do you want" said the Dragon." Well I have an extra room you could sleep in for the night." ;sugested the fox" and we could catch a squirrel for supper." "OK." said the Dragon. So the fox went out to catch sammy. Sammy went down to the pond to get some seeds when the fox saw Sammy he ran as fast as he could.

79 *Viewer Support Materials*

```
            The fox knew Sammy didn't like water so he

    would be trapec.  When they reached the pond Sammy
                                                    the
    jumped to the side and the fox went spashing in ~~re~~

    pond.  "I'll get you for this" yelled the fox as

    sammy ran up a tree.  Sammy# lived a very long

    life.
```

Biographical Sketches:

Guest Experts

(In Alphabetical Order)

Glenda Bissex entitled the write-up of the longitudinal study of her son Paul's growth into literacy, *GYNS AT WRK: A Child Learns to Write and Read.* She went on to explain to readers the significance of Paul's message and why she had selected it as the title of her book. "When he was five and a half years old, Paul wrote and posted this sign over his workbench-desk: DO NAT DSTRB GNYS AT WRK. The GNYS (genius) at work is our human capacity for language. DO NAT DSTRB is a caution to observe how it works, for the logic by which we teach is not always the logic by which children learn."

In teaching, little things make a difference. **Carolyn Burke**, Professor of Reading in the Department of Language Education at Indiana University, is truly one of the brightest people education has had the good fortune to attract. A former first grade teacher, Carolyn's real strength is her ability to take what is currently known and apply it to classroom instruction. In a real sense Carolyn is a teacher's teacher, demonstrating how to orchestrate the 'how' and 'what' of teaching to improve curriculum through theoretical consistency.

Some people are doers. **Orin Cochran**, now Principal of David Livingston School in Winnipeg, Manitoba, took it upon himself to do something to improve reading and writing instruction in Canada. As he conducted workshops he asked for teachers who also wanted to do something different—to give up their current teaching positions and come with him to start a demonstration school in downtown Winnipeg. The result of his efforts is an entire school faculty actively attempting to apply what we currently know about language and language learning for the betterment of schools and children. Results have been dramatic.

Trevor Cairney was a visiting professor at Indiana University on sabbatical leave from Bathhurst, Australia, when the support materials for this videotape series were being written. Because of his work in Australia in reading and writing, his interest in what reading and writing relationships mean for instruction, and his interest in teacher education more generally, he was invited to edit the support materials in this videotape series. Viewers will be thankful for his contribution.

Kittye Copeland is a first grade teacher in Columbia, Missouri. Kittye does much to fuse reading and writing in her classroom. Many of the "extended literature activities" which she has developed have been published by the local teacher support group of which she is a member. Together with Kathryn Mitchell Pierce, an ethnographer who has spent the last year in her classroom, Kittye has been exploring what "the language arts curriculum" means from the perspective of the child.

Paul Crowley, 1983 winner of the Barry Sherman Outstanding Teacher Award from the Center for the

Expansion of Language and Thinking, is a junior high special education teacher in the Columbia, Missouri, Public Schools. In a recent workshop where he had younger pupils writing stories to the wordless books his students had produced, a beginning teacher commented as she watched, "But I don't understand, these kids aren't 'special education' students. How did they ever get that label? Didn't anyone ever really work with them?" Paul knows only too well that anyone can intimidate a language learner. The program he has developed supports the language learner. His sensitivity is contagious. Not only will teachers identify with him, but they will want to emulate him.

Diane DeFord is an Associate Professor at The Ohio State University in Columbus, Ohio. Diane has done extensive research in classrooms studying how teacher expectancies, beliefs and behaviors affect student expectancies, beliefs and strategies in reading and writing. Her program of research clearly shows that what teachers believe about language and how it is learned makes a big instructional difference.

Carole Edelsky is an Associate Professor of Elementary Education at Arizona State University where she teaches courses in language arts, qualitative research, and sociolinguistics. Carole has done collaborative research in bilingual classrooms and sees the need for teachers to establish "authentic" language learning environments, and for researchers and teachers to stop acting as if all language information were equal.

Some people end up having been right more often than wrong. **Kenneth Goodman**, known affectionately as "Dr. God" to many in the profession, is one of the founding fathers of a psycholinguistic perspective on reading. His on-going research and insight into the process of reading led the National Council of Teachers of English to give him the David H. Russell Award for Distinguished Research in the Teaching of English in 1975. As past president of the International Reading Association, Ken was an eloquent spokesperson, reminding teachers, children, and fellow researchers that "there is nothing more basic than meaning in language."

Yetta Goodman, winner of the 1983−1984 International Reading Association's Outstanding Teacher Educator Award and past president of the National Council of Teachers of English, is a dynamic and much sought-after speaker. A former classroom teacher, Yetta is dedicated to improving public school education for all children, including children of minority groups. Recently Yetta and her colleagues have completed a reading and writing research project in classrooms on the Navajo reservation. Her concern, then, as always, has been "curriculum" which she feels all too often gets lost and misplaced. This concern includes reading educators' recent interest in writing, and a hope that writing will not become "yet another reading bandwagon."

Donald Graves has set new standards for research in education. He left the laboratory to go to the classroom, and he went not to watch teachers, but rather to work collaboratively with them. To make things even worse for researchers, he wrote his final research report so that teachers could read it! In doing all this, he literally put the University of New Hampshire on the map of reading and writing centers in the U.S., and made Atkinson Academy, a little, out-of-the-way place, one of the most exciting schools in the nation. His project is testimony to the fact that no matter where you are, there are things to be done, and golden opportunities ahead for the teaching of reading and writing. The National Council of Teachers of English honored Don by awarding him the David H. Russell Award for Distinguished Research in the Teaching of English in 1982 for his on-going contributions to our understanding of the writing process.

An author of children's books—*It Didn't Frighten Me, My Icky Picky Sister*, and others (School Book Fairs)—**Jerome Harste**'s writings range widely. As host and developer of this videotape series, Jerry has recently completed with Drs. Carolyn Burke and Virginia Woodward, a 7-year study of what preschool children, ages 3, 4, 5, and 6, know about reading and writing. Their book, *Language Stories & Literacy Lessons*, elaborates the theoretical base underlying the series and is recommended reading for teachers and teacher educators. This series extends that work by taking the insights gleaned into the processes of literacy and literacy learning to classroom instruction. Together with Dr. Pamela Terry and Philip Harris, Jerry is currently funded by the United States Department of Education to review the status of reading comprehension research for purposes of improving reading instruction. The particular focus of this latter project is special education.

Literacy is everyone's business. Rather than talk about the status of literacy to parents, **Patricia Jenkins**, Assistant Director of Special Education in the Columbia Public Schools, helped organize a Parents and Reading Fair. Children were introduced to the complete works of an author in school and invited to bring their parents, grandparents, and siblings with them to meet the author one evening after school. At the Fair, parents were shown how they could extend literature via their participation in hands-on child/parent workshops, and given the opportunity to help their child start an autographed collection of books for him or herself. The Parents and Reading Fair was a huge success both in terms of interest (over 600 parents and children attended) and the ownership of literacy it created among parents and children.

Martha King has spent a good share of her life convincing reading educators that "reading *is* a part of language." As is evident, the influence of her viewpoint has been felt. Martha has been involved in many research projects. Once, when Ohio State University had received a research grant to improve the teaching of reading comprehension, she convinced her research colleagues that they should pit their instructional interventions against classrooms in which children were free to just read widely. The control group—those who received no direct instruction but rather spent their time in the library reading widely—out-performed the treatment group on many reading comprehension measures! Martha is one of the "grand ladies" in reading and childhood education, never having lost her deep abiding respect for children and teachers.

Vera Milz is a classroom teacher at the Way Elementary School in Bloomfield Hills, Michigan. Dr. Milz recently completed her dissertation research on the subject of how first graders in her own classroom learned to write. As a practicing teacher-researcher and winner of the 1984 Barry Sherman Outstanding Teacher Award, she is actively involved in building a practical theory of literacy learning as it relates to language arts instruction.

P. David Pearson is Professor of Reading Education and Chairperson of the Department of Elementary Education at the University of Illinois. David has done extensive research in the area of reading, been co-editor of the *Reading Research Quarterly*, and while too modest to say so himself, is generally known as "Mr. Reading Comprehension" in the field of reading education.

Kathryn Mitchell Pierce currently teaches at Maryville College in St. Louis, Missouri. Having spent a year in Kittye Copeland's classroom, Kassi is completing her dissertation at Indiana University on the topic of curriculum as viewed from the perspective of the child. As a classroom teacher, Kassi's real strength was her ability to move theory to practice and hence was asked to help write up and edit the support materials in this videotape series.

Susan Robinson is a 6th grade teacher in the Indianapolis Public Schools. School 39, the school at which Sue taught for the past 8 years, serves an inner-city population of students. Sue has an easy-going personality. Her classroom is truly child-centered. In many ways she knows more about teaching than most. She knows just how much to plan, just when to make an invitation, and just when to back off to let students take ownership of both their projects and the classroom itself. She is one of the featured teachers in this videotape series. She is a marvel to watch. Sue was named Teacher of the Year in 1984 by the Indianapolis Public Schools. Her principal, Mr. Bennet, was named Administrator of the Year.

Olga Scribior, a classroom ethnographer from Halifax, Nova Scotia, spent one year in Myriam Revel-Wood's classroom studying children's growth in literacy as a function of their involvement in a comprehension-centered reading and writing program. Her report documents the social nature of language learning and how it is that the strategies of instruction become the strategies of literacy use. Olga currently teaches at Mount Saint Vincent University in Halifax.

The fields of reading and writing had become multidisciplinary rather than interdisciplinary. To help solve this problem **Nancy Shanklin**, University of Colorado-Denver, took it upon herself to apply recent insights from linguistics, sociolinguistics, cognitive psychology, education, literary criticism, cultural anthropology, philosophical linguistics, and semiotics to the study of literacy. Her transactional model of reading and writing suggests new instructional relationships and has been heralded as "one of the most significant contributions to the literature in the 80s."

While a good language arts program ought to include a wide variety of reading materials, good literature is certainly a key. Arguing that it's important that children meet authors, and that minority children meet minority authors, **Rudine Sims** brings her interest in multicultural education and children's literature to bear directly on the issue of setting up a comprehension-centered reading and writing program. An active leader in the National Council of Teachers of English, President of the Center for the Expansion of Language and Thinking, and Professor of Education at the University of Massachusetts, Rudine is a much sought after spokesperson for the profession.

Robert J. Tierney is a senior scientist at the Center for the Study of Reading at the University of Illinois. Over the past few years his major interest has focused upon the nature of reading and writing relationships. Rob has argued that, from the perspective of what the mind does, both reading and writing are "composing." His position raises the issue that, by having stated our interest in the form of the question, "What is the relationship between reading and writing?," we may have been setting ourselves up not to explore cognitive universals across these processes. One is reminded of Anthony Jay's famous statement that "the uncreative mind can spot wrong answers, but it takes a creative mind to spot wrong questions."

"Accent the positive . . . take that first step." This advice is good for children as well as for teachers. Dr. **Dorothy Watson**, Professor of Education at the University of Missouri-Columbia, is well known as a teacher educator for her ability to move teachers and schools. A former Kansas City classroom teacher, Dorothy is less interested in the past sins of omission and commission on the part of teachers than she is interested in the fact that "tomorrow is a new day." "There's nothing you have to be ashamed about," she tells teachers, "I did it once too . . . but, we now know better." She encourages teachers, like she encourages children, to begin where they are at . . . to take that first step. Understanding that when teachers are doing something new it is often "lonely out there," Dorothy has been instrumental in creating teacher support groups which meet once a month to eat, discuss, share, and generally support each other in the process of change. From Columbia, this program has grown. Currently there are teacher support groups throughout the United States and Canada.

Myriam Revel-Wood, one of the featured teachers in this videotape series, has spent the last 16 years teaching at University Elementary School in Bloomington, Indiana. University Elementary School is a public elementary school serving a wide range of socioeconomic and cultural groups. Last year 8 of the children in her classroom spoke little or no English at the beginning of the year. A native of Uruguay, Myriam travels widely and uses her love of science and social studies to open new worlds to the children. As a classroom teacher, Myriam's real forte is her deep understanding that our interest and our children's interest in reading and writing is an interest in learning. Hers is an exciting classroom. She opens new vistas for children, and they love her for it.

Mary Lynn Woods has spent fourteen years involved in classroom teaching experiences extending from preschool to college and reaching from Illinois to Ethiopia. The last 6 years she has been employed as a reading consultant, teacher, and Chapter I Director for the Eagle-Union Community Schools in Zionsville, Indiana. Mary Lynn has been actively involved in moving theory to practice. As one of the featured classroom teachers in this videotape series, Mary Lynn's particular strength is her ability to "think and extend curriculum" not only for children, but also for administrators and parents. Her leadership abilities make her a true asset to her school corporation.